Writings from the Zen Masters

Wumen Huikai
1183–1260

Kaku-an Shi-en
twelfth century

Mujū Dōkyō
1227–1312

Writings from the Zen Masters

COMPILED BY PAUL REPS

PENGUIN BOOKS — GREAT IDEAS

PENGUIN BOOKS

Published by the Penguin Group
Penguin Books Ltd, 80 Strand, London WC2R 0RL, England
Penguin Group (USA) Inc., 375 Hudson Street, New York, New York 10014, USA
Penguin Group (Canada), 90 Eglinton Avenue East, Suite 700, Toronto, Ontario, Canada M4P 2Y3
(a division of Pearson Penguin Canada Inc.)
Penguin Ireland, 25 St Stephen's Green, Dublin 2, Ireland
(a division of Penguin Books Ltd)
Penguin Group (Australia), 250 Camberwell Road, Camberwell, Victoria 3124, Australia
(a division of Pearson Australia Group Pty Ltd)
Penguin Books India Pvt Ltd, 11 Community Centre, Panchsheel Park, New Delhi – 110 017, India
Penguin Group (NZ), 67 Apollo Drive, Rosedale, North Shore 0632, New Zealand
(a division of Pearson New Zealand Ltd)
Penguin Books (South Africa) (Pty) Ltd, 24 Sturdee Avenue,
Rosebank, Johannesburg 2196, South Africa

Penguin Books Ltd, Registered Offices: 80 Strand, London WC2R 0RL, England

www.penguin.com

Taken from *Zen Flesh, Zen Bones* first published by Charles E. Tuttle & Co. Inc. 1957
This selection first published in Penguin Books 2009

003

Translation copyright © Charles E. Tuttle & Co. Inc. 1957
All rights reserved

All material transcribed by Nyogen Senzaki and Paul Reps.
Illustrations to 'Ten Bulls' by Tomikichiro Tokuriki
Published non-exclusively in Canada and by arrangement with Periplus Editions

Set by Rowland Phototypesetting Ltd, Bury St Edmunds, Suffolk
Printed in England by Clays Ltd, St Ives plc

978-0-141-04384-5

www.greenpenguin.co.uk

Penguin Books is committed to a sustainable
future for our business, our readers and our planet.
This book is made from Forest Stewardship
Council™ certified paper.

ALWAYS LEARNING   **PEARSON**

Contents

The Gateless Gate

By Ekai, called Mumon Wumen Huikai

'Zen has no gates. The purpose of Buddha's words is to enlighten others. Therefore Zen should be gateless.

'Now, how does one pass through this gateless gate? Some say that whatever enters through a gate is not family treasure, that whatever is produced by the help of another is likely to dissolve and perish.

'Even such words are like raising waves in a windless sea or performing an operation upon a healthy body. If one clings to what others have said and tries to understand Zen by explanation, he is like a dunce who thinks he can beat the moon with a pole or scratch an itching foot from the outside of a shoe. It will be impossible after all.

'In the year 1228 I was lecturing monks in the Ryusho temple in eastern China, and at their request I retold old koans, endeavouring to inspire their Zen spirit. I meant to use the koans as a man who picks up a piece of brick to knock at a gate, and after the gate is opened the brick is useless and is thrown away. My notes, however, were collected unexpectedly, and there were forty-nine koans, together with my comment in prose and verse concerning each, although their arrangement was not in the order of the telling. I have called the book The Gateless Gate, wishing students to read it as a guide.

'If a reader is brave enough and goes straight forward in his meditation, no delusions can disturb him. He will become enlightened just as did the patriarchs in India and in China, *probably even better. But if he hesitates one moment, he is as a person watching from a small window for a horseman to pass by, and in a wink he has missed seeing.*

> 'The great path has no gates,
> Thousands of roads enter it.
> When one passes through this gateless gate
> He walks freely between heaven and earth.'

狗 1. Joshu's Dog

A monk asked Joshu, a Chinese Zen master: 'Has a dog Buddha-nature or not?'

Joshu answered: 'Mu.' [Mu is the negative symbol in Chinese, meaning 'No-thing' or 'Nay'.]

Mumon's comment: To realize Zen one has to pass through the barrier of the patriarchs. Enlightenment always comes after the road of thinking is blocked. If you do not pass the barrier of the patriarchs or if your thinking road is not blocked, whatever you think, whatever you do, is like a tangling ghost. You may ask: What is a barrier of a patriarch? This one word, Mu, is it.

This is the barrier of Zen. If you pass through it you will see Joshu face to face. Then you can work hand in hand with the whole line of patriarchs. Is this not a pleasant thing to do?

If you want to pass this barrier, you must work through every bone in your body, through every pore of your skin, filled with this question: What is Mu? and carry it day and night. Do not believe it is the common negative symbol meaning nothing. It is not nothingness, the opposite of existence. If you really want to pass this barrier, you should feel like drinking a hot iron ball that you can neither swallow nor spit out.

Then your previous lesser knowledge disappears. As a

fruit ripening in season, your subjectivity and objectivity naturally become one. It is like a dumb man who has had a dream. He knows about it but he cannot tell it.

When he enters this condition his ego-shell is crushed and he can shake the heaven and move the earth. He is like a great warrior with a sharp sword. If a Buddha stands in his way, he will cut him down; if a patriarch offers him any obstacle, he will kill him; and he will be free in his way of birth and death. He can enter any world as if it were his own playground. I will tell you how to do this with this koan:

Just concentrate your whole energy into this Mu, and do not allow any discontinuation. When you enter this Mu and there is no discontinuation, your attainment will be as a candle burning and illuminating the whole universe.

Has a dog Buddha-nature?
This is the most serious question of all.
If you say yes or no,
You lose your own Buddha-nature.

狐 2. Hyakujo's Fox

Once when Hyakujo delivered some Zen lectures an old man attended them, unseen by the monks. At the end of each talk when the monks left so did he. But one day he remained after they had gone, and Hyakujo asked him: 'Who are you?'

The old man replied: 'I am not a human being, but I was a human being when the Kashapa Buddha preached in this world. I was a Zen master and lived on this mountain. At that time one of my students asked me whether or not the enlightened man is subject to the law of causation. I answered him: "The enlightened man is not subject to the law of causation." For this answer evidencing a clinging to absoluteness I became a fox for five hundred rebirths, and I am still a fox. Will you save me from this condition with your Zen words and let me get out of a fox's body? Now may I ask you: Is the enlightened man subject to the law of causation?'

Hyakujo said: 'The enlightened man is one with the law of causation.'

At the words of Hyakujo the old man was enlightened. 'I am emancipated,' he said, paying homage with a deep bow. 'I am no more a fox, but I have to leave my body in my dwelling place behind this mountain. Please perform my funeral as a monk.' Then he disappeared.

The next day Hyakujo gave an order through the chief

monk to prepare to attend the funeral of a monk. 'No one was sick in the infirmary,' wondered the monks. 'What does our teacher mean?'

After dinner Hyakujo led the monks out and around the mountain. In a cave, with his staff he poked out the corpse of an old fox and then performed the ceremony of cremation.

That evening Hyakujo gave a talk to the monks and told them this story about the law of causation.

Obaku, upon hearing the story, asked Hyakujo: 'I understand that a long time ago because a certain person gave a wrong Zen answer he became a fox for five hundred rebirths. Now I want to ask: If some modern master is asked many questions and he always gives the right answer, what will become of him?'

Hyakujo said: 'You come here near me and I will tell you.'

Obaku went near Hyakujo and slapped the teacher's face with his hand, for he knew this was the answer his teacher intended to give him.

Hyakujo clapped his hands and laughed at this discernment. 'I thought a Persian had a red beard,' he said, 'and now I know a Persian who has a red beard.'

Mumon's comment: 'The enlightened man is not subject.' How can this answer make the monk a fox?

'The enlightened man is one with the law of causation.' How can this answer make the fox emancipated?

To understand this clearly one has to have just one eye.

The Gateless Gate

Controlled or not controlled?
The same dice shows two faces.
Not controlled or controlled,
Both are a grievous error.

指 3. Gutei's Finger

Gutei raised his finger whenever he was asked a question about Zen. A boy attendant began to imitate him in this way. When anyone asked the boy what his master had preached about, the boy would raise his finger.

Gutei heard about the boy's mischief. He seized him and cut off his finger. The boy cried and ran away. Gutei called and stopped him. When the boy turned his head to Gutei, Gutei raised up his own finger. In that instant the boy was enlightened.

When Gutei was about to pass from this world he gathered his monks around him. 'I attained my finger-Zen,' he said, 'from my teacher Tenryu, and in my whole life I could not exhaust it.' Then he passed away.

Mumon's comment: Enlightenment, which Gutei and the boy attained, has nothing to do with a finger. If anyone clings to a finger, Tenryu will be so disappointed that he will annihilate Gutei, the boy and the clinger all together.

> *Gutei cheapens the teaching of Tenryu,*
> *Emancipating the boy with a knife.*
> *Compared to the Chinese god who pushed*
>   *aside a mountain with one hand*
> *Old Gutei is a poor imitator.*

異 4. *A Beardless Foreigner*

Wakuan complained when he saw a picture of beardless Bodhidharma: 'Why hasn't that fellow a beard?'

Mumon's comment: If you want to study Zen, you must study it with your heart. When you attain realization, it must be true realization. You yourself must have the face of the great Bodhidharma to see him. Just one such glimpse will be enough. But if you say you met him, you never saw him at all.

> One should not discuss a dream
> In front of a simpleton.
> Why has Bodhidharma no beard?
> What an absurd question!

落 5. *Kyogen Mounts the Tree*

Kyogen said: 'Zen is like a man hanging in a tree by his teeth over a precipice. His hands grasp no branch, his feet rest on no limb, and under the tree another person asks him: 'Why did Bodhidharma come to China from India?'

'If the man in the tree does not answer, he fails; and if he does answer, he falls and loses his life. Now what shall he do?'

Mumon's comment: In such a predicament the most talented eloquence is of no use. If you have memorized all the sutras, you cannot use them. When you can give the right answer, even though your past road was one of death, you open up a new road of life. But if you cannot answer, you should live ages hence and ask the future Buddha, Maitreya.

> *Kyogen is truly a fool*
> *Spreading that ego-killing poison*
> *That closes his pupils' mouths*
> *And lets their tears stream from*
>   *their dead eyes.*

形 6. Buddha Twirls a Flower

When Buddha was in Grdhrakuta mountain he turned a flower in his fingers and held it before his listeners. Every one was silent. Only Maha-Kashapa smiled at this revelation, although he tried to control the lines of his face.

Buddha said: 'I have the eye of the true teaching, the heart of Nirvana, the true aspect of non-form, and the ineffable stride of Dharma. It is not expressed by words, but especially transmitted beyond teaching. This teaching I have given to Maha-Kashapa.'

Mumon's comment: Golden-faced Gautama thought he could cheat anyone. He made the good listeners as bad, and sold dog meat under the sign of mutton. And he himself thought it was wonderful. What if all the audience had laughed together? How could he have transmitted the teaching? And again, if Maha-Kashapa had not smiled, how could he have transmitted the teaching? If he says that realization can be transmitted, he is like the city slicker that cheats the country dub, and if he says it cannot be transmitted, why does he approve of Maha-Kashapa?

> *At the turning of a flower*
> *His disguise was exposed.*
> *No one in heaven or earth can surpass*
> *Maha-Kashapa's wrinkled face.*

洗 *7. Joshu Washes the Bowl*

A monk told Joshu: 'I have just entered the monastery. Please teach me.'
   Joshu asked: 'Have you eaten your rice porridge?'
   The monk replied: 'I have eaten.'
   Joshu said: 'Then you had better wash your bowl.'
   At that moment the monk was enlightened.

Mumon's comment: Joshu is the man who opens his mouth and shows his heart. I doubt if this monk really saw Joshu's heart. I hope he did not mistake the bell for a pitcher.

> *It is too clear and so it is hard to see.*
> *A dunce once searched for a fire with a*
> *   lighted lantern.*
> *Had he known what fire was,*
> *He could have cooked his rice much sooner.*

輪 8. Keichu's Wheel

Getsuan said to his students: 'Keichu, the first wheel-maker of China, made two wheels of fifty spokes each. Now, suppose you removed the nave uniting the spokes. What would become of the wheel? And had Keichu done this, could he be called the master wheel-maker?'

Mumon's comment: If anyone can answer this question instantly, his eyes will be like a comet and his mind like a flash of lightning.

> *When the hubless wheel turns,*
> *Master or no master can stop it.*
> *It turns above heaven and below earth,*
> *South, north, east and west.*

聖 *9. A Buddha Before History*

A monk asked Seijo: 'I understand that a Buddha who lived before recorded history sat in meditation for ten cycles of existence and could not realize the highest truth, and so could not become fully emancipated. Why was this so?'

Seijo replied: 'Your question is self-explanatory.'

The monk asked: 'Since the Buddha was meditating, why could he not fulfill Buddahood?'

Seijo said: 'He was not a Buddha.'

Mumon's comment: I will allow his realization, but I will not admit his understanding. When one ignorant attains realization he is a saint. When a saint begins to understand he is ignorant.

> *It is better to realize mind than body.*
> *When mind is realized one need not worry*
>   *about body.*
> *When mind and body become one*
> *The man is free. Then he desires no praising.*

貪 10. *Seizei Alone and Poor*

A monk named Seizei asked of Sozan: 'Seizei is alone and poor. Will you give him support?'

Sozan asked: 'Seizei?'

Seizei responded: 'Yes, sir.'

Sozan said: 'You have Zen, the best wine in China, and already have finished three cups, and still you are saying that they did not even wet your lips.'

Mumon's comment: Seizei overplayed his hand. Why was it so? Because Sozan had eyes and knew with whom to deal. Even so, I want to ask: At what point did Seizei drink wine?

> *The poorest man in China,*
> *The bravest man in China,*
> *He barely sustains himself,*
> *Yet wishes to rival the wealthiest.*

想
念

11. *Joshu Examines a Monk in Meditation*

Joshu went to a place where a monk had retired to meditate and asked him: 'What is, is what?'

The monk raised his fist.

Joshu replied: 'Ships cannot remain where the water is too shallow.' And he left.

A few days later Joshu went again to visit the monk and asked the same question.

The monk answered the same way.

Joshu said: 'Well given, well taken, well killed, well saved.' And he bowed to the monk.

Mumon's comment: The raised fist was the same both times. Why is it Joshu did not admit the first and approved the second one? Where is the fault?

Whoever answers this knows that Joshu's tongue has no bone so he can use it freely. Yet perhaps Joshu is wrong. Or, through that monk, he may have discovered his mistake.

If anyone thinks that the one's insight exceeds the other's, he has no eyes.

> *The light of the eyes is as a comet,*
> *And Zen's activity is as lightning.*
> *The sword that kills the man*
> *Is the sword that saves the man.*

誤 12. *Zuigan Calls His Own Master*

Zuigan called out to himself every day: 'Master.'
  Then he answered himself: 'Yes, sir.'
  And after that he added: 'Become sober.'
  Again he answered: 'Yes, sir.'
  'And after that,' he continued, 'do not be deceived by others.'
  'Yes, sir; yes, sir,' he answered.

Mumon's comment: Old Zuigan sells out and buys himself. He is opening a puppet show. He uses one mask to call 'Master' and another that answers the master. Another mask says 'Sober up' and another, 'Do not be cheated by others.' If anyone clings to any of his masks, he is mistaken, yet if he imitates Zuigan, he will make himself fox-like.

> *Some Zen students do not realize the true*
>   *man in a mask*
> *Because they recognize ego-soul.*
> *Ego-soul is the seed of birth and death,*
> *And foolish people call it the true man.*

椀 13. Tokusan Holds His Bowl

Tokusan went to the dining room from the meditation hall holding his bowl. Seppo was on duty cooking. When he met Tokusan he said: 'The dinner drum is not yet beaten. Where are you going with your bowl?'

So Tokusan returned to his room.

Seppo told Ganto about this. Ganto said: 'Old Tokusan did not understand ultimate truth.'

Tokusan heard of this remark and asked Ganto to come to him. 'I have heard,' he said, 'you are not approving my Zen.' Ganto admitted this indirectly. Tokusan said nothing.

The next day Tokusan delivered an entirely different kind of lecture to the monks. Ganto laughed and clapped his hands, saying: 'I see our old man understands ultimate truth indeed. None in China can surpass him.'

Mumon's comment: Speaking about ultimate truth, both Ganto and Tokusan did not even dream it. After all, they are dummies.

> *Whoever understands the first truth*
> *Should understand the ultimate truth.*
> *The last and first,*
> *Are they not the same?*

斷 14. *Nansen Cuts the Cat in Two*

Nansen saw the monks of the eastern and western halls fighting over a cat. He seized the cat and told the monks: 'If any of you say a good word, you can save the cat.'

No one answered. So Nansen boldly cut the cat in two pieces.

That evening Joshu returned and Nansen told him about this. Joshu removed his sandals and, placing them on his head, walked out.

Nansen said: 'If you had been there, you could have saved the cat.'

Mumon's comment: Why did Joshu put his sandals on his head? If anyone answers this question, he will understand exactly how Nansen enforced the edict. If not, he should watch his own head.

> *Had Joshu been there,*
> *He would have enforced the edict oppositely.*
> *Joshua snatches the sword*
> *And Nansen begs for his life.*

質 15. Tozan's Three Blows

Tozan went to Ummon. Ummon asked him where he had come from.

Tozan said: 'From Sato village.'

Ummon asked: 'In what temple did you remain for the summer?'

Tozan replied: 'The temple of Hoji, south of the lake.'

'When did you leave there?' asked Ummon, wondering how long Tozan would continue with such factual answers.

'The twenty-fifth of August,' answered Tozan.

Ummon said: 'I should give you three blows with a stick, but today I forgive you.'

The next day Tozan bowed to Ummon and asked: 'Yesterday you forgave me three blows. I do not know why you thought me wrong.'

Ummon, rebuking Tozan's spiritless responses, said: 'You are good for nothing. You simply wander from one monastery to another.'

Before Ummon's words were ended Tozan was enlightened.

Mumon's comment: Ummon fed Tozan good Zen food. If Tozan can digest it, Ummon may add another member to his family.

In the evening Tozan swam around in a sea of good

22

and bad, but at dawn Ummon crushed his nut shell. After all, he wasn't so smart.

Now, I want to ask: Did Tozan deserve the three blows? If you say yes, not only Tozan but every one of you deserves them. If you say no, Ummon is speaking a lie. If you answer this question clearly, you can eat the same food as Tozan.

> *The lioness teaches her cubs roughly;*
> *The cubs jump and she knocks them down.*
> *When Ummon saw Tozan his first arrow was light;*
> *His second arrow shot deep.*

鐘 16. *Bells and Robes*

Ummon asked: 'The world is such a wide world, why do you answer a bell and don ceremonial robes?'

Mumon's comment: When one studies Zen one need not follow sound or colour or form. Even though some have attained insight when hearing a voice or seeing a colour or a form, this is a very common way. It is not true Zen. The real Zen student controls sound, colour, form, and actualizes the truth in his everyday life.

Sound comes to the ear, the ear goes to sound. When you blot out sound and sense, what do you understand? While listening with ears one never can understand. To understand intimately one should see sound.

> *When you understand, you belong to the family;*
> *When you do not understand, you are a stranger.*
> *Those who do not understand belong to the family,*
> *And when they understand they are strangers.*

汳
荅

17. The Three Calls of the Emperor's Teacher

Chu, called Kokushi, the teacher of the emperor, called to his attendant: 'Oshin.'

Oshin answered: 'Yes.'

Chu repeated, to test his pupil: 'Oshin.'

Oshin repeated: 'Yes.'

Chu called: 'Oshin.'

Oshin answered: 'Yes.'

Chu said: 'I ought to apologize to you for all this calling, but really you ought to apologize to me.'

Mumon's comment: When Old Chu called Oshin three times his tongue was rotting, but when Oshin answered three times his words were brilliant. Chu was getting decrepit and lonesome, and his method of teaching was like holding a cow's head to feed it clover.

Oshin did not trouble to show his Zen either. His satisfied stomach had no desire to feast. When the country is prosperous everyone is indolent; when the home is wealthy the children are spoiled.

Now I want to ask you: Which one should apologize?

> When prison stocks are iron and have no
> place for the head, the prisoner is doubly
> in trouble.

Wumen Huikai

When there is no place for Zen in the head of our
*   generation, it is in grievous trouble.*
If you try to hold up the gate and door of a falling house,
You also will be in trouble.

量 18. Tozan's Three Pounds

A monk asked Tozan when he was weighing some flax: 'What is Buddha?'

Tozan said: 'This flax weighs three pounds.'

Mumon's comment: Old Tozan's Zen is like a clam. The minute the shell opens you see the whole inside. However, I want to ask you: Do you see the real Tozan?

> *Three pounds of flax in front of your nose,*
> *Close enough, and mind is still closer.*
> *Whoever talks about affirmation and negation*
> *Lives in the right and wrong region.*

常 19. *Everyday Life is the Path*

Joshu asked Nansen: 'What is the path?'

Nansen said: 'Everyday life is the path.'

Joshu asked: 'Can it be studied?'

Nansen said: 'If you try to study, you will be far away from it.'

Joshu asked: 'If I do not study, how can I know it is the path?'

Nansen said: 'The path does not belong to the perception world, neither does it belong to the nonperception world. Cognition is a delusion and noncognition is senseless. If you want to reach the true path beyond doubt, place yourself in the same freedom as sky. You name it neither good nor not-good.'

At these words Joshu was enlightened.

Mumon's comment: Nansen could melt Joshu's frozen doubts at once when Joshu asked his questions. I doubt though if Joshu reached the point that Nansen did. He needed thirty more years of study.

In spring, hundreds of flowers; in autumn, a harvest moon;
In summer, a refreshing breeze; in winter, snow will
accompany you.
If useless things do not hang in your mind,
Any season is a good season for you.

綴 20. The Enlightened Man

Shogen asked: 'Why does the enlightened man not stand on his feet and explain himself?' And he also said: 'It is not necessary for speech to come from the tongue.'

Mumon's comment: Shogen spoke plainly enough, but how many will understand? If anyone comprehends, he should come to my place and test out my big stick. Why, look here, to test real gold you must see it through fire.

> If the feet of enlightenment moved, the great
> ocean would overflow;
> If that head bowed, it would look down upon
> the heavens.
> Such a body has no place to rest . . .
> Let another continue this poem.

塵 21. Dried Dung

A monk asked Ummon: 'What is Buddha?' Ummon answered him: 'Dried dung.'

Mumon's comment: It seems to me Ummon is so poor he cannot distinguish the taste of one food from another, or else he is too busy to write readable letters. Well, he tried to hold his school with dried dung. And his teaching was just as useless.

> *Lightning flashes,*
> *Sparks shower.*
> *In one blink of your eyes*
> *You have missed seeing.*

弟 22. Kashapa's Preaching Sign

Ananda asked Kashapa: 'Buddha gave you the golden-woven robe of successorship. What else did he give you?'

Kashapa said: 'Ananda.'

Ananda answered: 'Yes, brother.'

Said Kashapa: 'Now you can take down my preaching sign and put up your own.'

Mumon's comment: If one understands this, he will see the old brotherhood still gathering, but if not, even though he has studied the truth from ages before the Buddhas, he will not attain enlightenment.

> *The point of the question is dull but the answer is intimate.*
> *How many persons hearing it will open their eyes?*
> *Elder brother calls and younger brother answers,*
> *This spring does not belong to the ordinary season.*

不孝 23. Do Not Think Good, Do Not Think Not-Good

When he became emancipated the sixth patriarch received from the fifth patriarch the bowl and robe given from the Buddha to his successors, generation after generation.

A monk named E-myo out of envy pursued the patriarch to take this great treasure away from him. The sixth patriarch placed the bowl and robe on a stone in the road and told E-myo: 'These objects just symbolize the faith. There is no use fighting over them. If you desire to take them, take them now.'

When E-myo went to move the bowl and robe they were as heavy as mountains. He could not budge them. Trembling for shame he said: 'I came wanting the teaching, not the material treasures. Please teach me.'

The sixth patriarch said: 'When you do not think good and when you do not think not-good, what is your true self?'

At these words E-myo was illumined. Perspiration broke out all over his body. He cried and bowed, saying: 'You have given me the secret words and meanings. Is there yet a deeper part of the teaching?'

The sixth patriarch replied: 'What I have told you is no secret at all. When you realize your own true self the secret belongs to you.'

E-myo said: 'I was under the fifth patriarch many years

but could not realize my true self until now. Through your teaching I find the source. A person drinks water and knows himself whether it is cold or warm. May I call you my teacher?'

The sixth patriarch replied: 'We studied together under the fifth patriarch. Call him your teacher, but just treasure what you have attained.'

Mumon's comments: The sixth patriarch certainly was kind in such an emergency. It was as if he removed the skin and seeds from the fruit and then, opening the pupil's mouth, let him eat.

> *You cannot describe it, you cannot picture it,*
> *You cannot admire it, you cannot sense it.*
> *It is your true self, it has nowhere to hide.*
> *When the world is destroyed, it will not be destroyed.*

去 24. *Without Words, Without Silence*

A monk asked Fuketsu: 'Without speaking, without silence, how can you express the truth?'

Fuketsu observed: 'I always remember spring-time in southern China. The birds sing among innumerable kinds of fragrant flowers.'

Mumon's comment: Fuketsu used to have lightning Zen. Whenever he had the opportunity, he flashed it. But this time he failed to do so and only borrowed from an old Chinese poem. Never mind Fuketsu's Zen. If you want to express the truth, throw out your words, throw out your silence, and tell me about your own Zen.

> *Without revealing his own penetration,*
> *He offered another's words, not his to give.*
> *Had he chattered on and on,*
> *Even his listeners would have been embarrassed.*

浮 25. *Preaching from the Third Seat*

In a dream Kyozan went to Maitreya's Pure Land. He recognized himself seated in the third seat in the abode of Maitreya. Someone announced: 'Today the one who sits in the third seat will preach.'

Kyozan arose and, hitting the gavel, said: 'The truth of Mahayana teaching is transcendent, above words and thought. Do you understand?'

Mumon's comment: I want to ask you monks: Did he preach or did he not?

When he opens his mouth he is lost. When he seals his mouth he is lost. If he does not open it, if he does not seal it, he is 108,000 miles from truth.

> *In the light of day,*
> *Yet in a dream he talks of a dream.*
> *A monster among monsters,*
> *He intended to deceive the whole crowd.*

薦 26. Two Monks Roll Up the Screen

Hogen of Seiryo monastery was about to lecture before dinner when he noticed that the bamboo screen lowered for meditation had not been rolled up. He pointed to it. Two monks arose from the audience and rolled it up.

Hogen, observing the physical moment, said: 'The state of the first monk is good, not that of the other.'

Mumon's comment: I want to ask you: Which of those two monks gained and which lost? If any of you has one eye, he will see the failure on the teacher's part. However, I am not discussing gain and loss.

> *When the screen is rolled up the great sky opens,*
> *Yet the sky is not attuned to Zen.*
> *It is best to forget the great sky*
> *And to retire from every wind.*

唯
無

27. It is Not Mind, It is Not Buddha, It is Not Things

A monk asked Nansen: 'Is there a teaching no master ever preached before?'

Nansen said: 'Yes, there is.'

'What is it?' asked the monk.

Nansen replied: 'It is not mind, it is not Buddha, it is not things.'

Mumon's comment: Old Nansen gave away his treasure-words. He must have been greatly upset.

> Nansen was too kind and lost his treasure.
> Truly, words have no power.
> Even though the mountain becomes the sea,
> Words cannot open another's mind.

灰 28. Blow Out the Candle

Tokusan was studying Zen under Ryutan. One night he came to Ryutan and asked many questions. The teacher said: 'The night is getting old. Why don't you retire?'

So Tokusan bowed and opened the screen to go out, observing: 'It is very dark outside.'

Ryutan offered Tokusan a lighted candle to find his way. Just as Tokusan received it, Ryutan blew it out. At that moment the mind of Tokusan was opened.

'What have you attained?' asked Ryutan.

'From now on,' said Tokusan, 'I will not doubt the teacher's words.'

The next day Ryutan told the monks at his lecture: 'I see one monk among you. His teeth are like the sword tree, his mouth is like the blood bowl. If you hit him hard with a big stick, he will not even so much as look back at you. Someday he will mount the highest peak and carry my teaching there.'

On that day, in front of the lecture hall, Tokusan burned to ashes his commentaries on the sutras. He said: 'However abstruse the teachings are, in comparison with this enlightenment they are like a single hair to the great sky. However profound the complicated knowledge of the world, compared to this enlightenment it is like one drop of water to the great ocean.' Then he left that monastery.

*

Mumon's comment: When Tokusan was in his own country he was not satisfied with Zen although he had heard about it. He thought: 'Those Southern monks say they can teach Dharma outside of the sutras. They are all wrong. I must teach them.' So he travelled south. He happened to stop near Ryutan's monastery for refreshments. An old woman who was there asked him: 'What are you carrying so heavily?'

Tokusan replied: 'This is a commentary I have made on the Diamond Sutra after many years of work.'

The old woman said: 'I read that sutra which says: "The past mind cannot be held, the present mind cannot be held." You wish some tea and refreshments. Which mind do you propose to use for them?'

Tokusan was as though dumb. Finally he asked the woman: 'Do you know of any good teacher around here?'

The old woman referred him to Ryutan, not more than five miles away. So he went to Ryutan in all humility, quite different from when he had started his journey. Ryutan in turn was so kind he forgot his own dignity. It was like pouring muddy water over a drunken man to sober him. After all, it was an unnecessary comedy.

> *A hundred hearings cannot surpass one seeing,*
> *But after you see the teacher, that one glance*
>   *cannot surpass a hundred hearings.*
> *His nose was very high*
> *But he was blind after all.*

⟨ℛⲉ⟩ 29. *Not the Wind, Not the Flag*

Two monks were arguing about a flag. One said: 'The flag is moving.'

The other said: 'The wind is moving.'

The sixth patriarch happened to be passing by. He told them: 'Not the wind, not the flag; mind is moving.'

Mumon's comment: The sixth patriarch said: 'The wind is not moving, the flag is not moving. Mind is moving.' What did he mean? If you understand this intimately, you will see the two monks there trying to buy iron and gaining gold. The sixth patriarch could not bear to see those two dull heads, so he made such a bargain.

> *Wind, flag, mind moves.*
> *The same understanding.*
> *When the mouth opens*
> *All are wrong.*

精 30. *This Mind is Buddha*

Daibai asked Baso: 'What is Buddha?'
  Baso said: 'This mind is Buddha.'

Mumon's comment: If anyone wholly understands this, he is wearing Buddha's clothing, he is eating Buddha's food, he is speaking Buddha's words, he is behaving as Buddha, he is Buddha.

This ancedote, however, has given many a pupil the sickness of formality. If one truly understands, he will wash out his mouth for three days after saying the word Buddha, and he will close his ears and flee after hearing 'This mind is Buddha.'

> *Under blue sky, in bright sunlight,*
> *One need not search around.*
> *Asking what Buddha is*
> *Is like hiding loot in one's pocket and*
>   *declaring oneself innocent.*

探 31. *Joshu Investigates*

A travelling monk asked an old woman the road to Taizan, a popular temple supposed to give wisdom to the one who worships there. The old woman said: 'Go straight ahead.' When the monk proceeded a few steps, she said to herself: 'He also is a common church-goer.'

Someone told this incident to Joshu, who said: 'Wait until I investigate.' The next day he went and asked the same question, and the old woman gave the same answer.

Joshu remarked: 'I have investigated that old woman.'

Mumon's comment: The old woman understood how war is planned, but she did not know how spies sneak in behind her tent. Old Joshu played the spy's work and turned the tables on her, but he was not an able general. Both had their faults. Now I want to ask you: What was the point of Joshu's investigating the old woman?

> *When the question is common*
> *The answer is also common.*
> *When the question is sand in a bowl of boiled rice*
> *The answer is a stick in the soft mud.*

㒼 32. A Philosopher Asks Buddha

A philosopher asked Buddha: 'Without words, without the wordless, will you tell me truth?'

The Buddha kept silence.

The philosopher bowed and thanked the Buddha, saying: 'With your loving kindness I have cleared away my delusions and entered the true path.'

After the philosopher had gone, Ananda asked the Buddha what he had attained.

The Buddha replied: 'A good horse runs even at the shadow of the whip.'

Mumon's comment: Ananda was the disciple of the Buddha. Even so, his opinion did not surpass that of outsiders. I want to ask you monks: How much difference is there between disciples and outsiders?

> *To tread the sharp edge of a sword*
> *To run on smooth-frozen ice,*
> *One needs no footsteps to follow.*
> *Walk over the cliffs with hands free.*

粹 *33. This Mind is Not Buddha*

A monk asked Baso: 'What is Buddha?'
Baso said: 'This mind is not Buddha.'

Mumon's comment: If anyone understands this, he is a graduate of Zen.

> *If you meet a fencing-master on the road, you*
> *may give him your sword,*
> *If you meet a poet, you may offer him your poem.*
> *When you meet others, say only a part of what*
> *you intend.*
> *Never give the whole thing at once.*

羞 *34. Learning is Not the Path*

Nansen said: 'Mind is not Buddha. Learning is not the path.'

Mumon's comment: Nansen was getting old and forgot to be ashamed. He spoke out with bad breath and exposed the scandal of his own home. However, there are few who appreciate his kindness.

> When the sky is clear the sun appears,
> When the earth is parched rain will fall.
> He opened his heart fully and spoke out,
> But it was useless to talk to pigs and fish.

双 35. *Two Souls*

'Seijo, the Chinese girl,' observed Goso, 'had two souls, one always sick at home and the other in the city, a married woman with two children. Which was the true soul?'

Mumon's comment: When one understands this, he will know it is possible to come out from one shell and enter another, as if one were stopping at a transient lodging house. But if he cannot understand, when his time comes and his four elements separate, he will be just like a crab dipped in boiling water, struggling with many hands and legs. In such a predicament he may say: 'Mumon did not tell me where to go!' but it will be too late then.

> *The moon above the clouds is the same moon,*
> *The mountains and rivers below are all different.*
> *Each is happy in its unity and variety.*
> *This is one, this is two.*

36. Meeting a Zen Master on the Road

Goso said: 'When you meet a Zen master on the road you cannot talk to him, you cannot face him with silence. What are you going to do?'

Mumon's comment: In such a case, if you can answer him intimately, your realization will be beautiful, but if you cannot, you should look about without seeing anything.

> Meeting a Zen master on the road,
> Face him neither with words nor silence.
> Give him an uppercut
> And you will be called one who understands Zen.

37. A Buffalo Passes Through the Enclosure

Goso said: 'When a buffalo goes out of his enclosure to the edge of the abyss, his horns and his head and his hoofs all pass through, but why can't the tail also pass?'

Mumon's comment: If anyone can open one eye at this point and say a word of Zen, he is qualified to repay the four gratifications, and, not only that, he can save all sentient beings under him. But if he cannot say such a word of true Zen, he should turn back to his tail.

> *If the buffalo runs, he will fall into the trench;*
> *If he returns, he will be butchered.*
> *That little tail*
> *Is a very strange thing.*

樫 38. An Oak Tree in the Garden

A monk asked Joshu why Bodhidharma came to China. Joshu said: 'An oak tree in the garden.'

Mumon's comment: If one sees Joshu's answer clearly, there is no Shakyamuni Buddha before him and no future Buddha after him.

> Words cannot describe everything.
> The heart's message cannot be delivered in words.
> If one receives words literally, he will be lost.
> If he tries to explain with words, he will not attain
>   enlightenment in this life.

㽞 39. Ummon's Sidetrack

A Zen student told Ummon: 'Brilliancy of Buddha illuminates the whole universe.'

Before he finished the phrase Ummon asked: 'You are reciting another's poem, are you not?'

'Yes,' answered the student.

'You are sidetracked,' said Ummon.

Afterwards another teacher, Shishin, asked his pupils: 'At what point did that student go off the track?'

Mumon's comment: If anyone perceives Ummon's particular skilfulness, he will know at what point the student was off the track, and he will be a teacher of man and Devas. If not, he cannot even perceive himself.

> *When a fish meets the fishhook*
> *If he is too greedy, he will be caught.*
> *When his mouth opens*
> *His life already is lost.*

壺 40. Tipping Over a Water Vase

Hyakujo wished to send a monk to open a new monastery. He told his pupils that whoever answered a question most ably would be appointed. Placing a water vase on the ground, he asked: 'Who can say what this is without calling its name?'

The chief monk said: 'No one can call it a wooden shoe.'

Isan, the cooking monk, tipped over the vase with his foot and went out.

Hyakujo smiled and said: 'The chief monk loses.' And Isan became the master of the new monastery.

Mumon's comment: Isan was brave enough, but he could not escape Hyakujo's trick. After all, he gave up a light job and took a heavy one. Why, can't you see, he took off his comfortable hat and placed himself in iron stocks.

> *Giving up cooking utensils,*
> *Defeating the chatterbox,*
> *Though his teacher sets a barrier for him*
> *His feet will tip over everything, even the Buddha.*

壁 41. Bodhidharma Pacifies the Mind

Bodhidharma sits facing the wall. His future successor stands in the snow and presents his severed arm to Bodhidharma. He cries: 'My mind is not pacified, pacify my mind.'

Bodhidharma says: 'If you bring me that mind, I will pacify it for you.'

The successor says: 'When I search my mind I cannot hold it.'

Bodhidharma says: 'Then your mind is pacified already.'

Mumon's comment: That broken-toothed old Hindu, Bodhidharma, came thousands of miles over the sea from India to China as if he had something wonderful. He is like raising waves without wind. After he remained years in China he had only one disciple and that one lost his arm and was deformed. Alas, ever since he has had brainless disciples.

> *Why did Bodhidharma come to China?*
> *For years monks have discussed this.*
> *All the troubles that have followed since*
> *Came from that teacher and disciple.*

生起 42. *The Girl Comes Out from Meditation*

In the time of Buddha Shakyamuni, Manjusri went to the assemblage of the Buddhas. When he arrived there, the conference was over and each Buddha had returned to his own Buddha-land. Only one girl was yet unmoved in deep meditation.

Manjusri asked Buddha Shakyamuni how it was possible for this girl to reach this state, one which even he could not attain. 'Bring her out from Samadhi and ask her yourself,' said the Buddha.

Manjusri walked around the girl three times and snapped his fingers. She still remained in meditation. So by his miracle power he transported her to a high heaven and tried his best to call her, but in vain.

Buddha Shakyamuni said: 'Even a hundred thousand Manjusris could not disturb her, but below this place past twelve hundred million countries, is a Bodhisattva, Mo-myo, seed of delusion. If he comes here, she will awaken.'

No sooner had the Buddha spoken than that Bodhisattva sprang up from the earth and bowed and paid homage to the Buddha. Buddha directed him to arouse the girl. The Bodhisattva went in front of the girl and snapped his fingers, and in that instant the girl came out from her deep meditation.

*

Mumon's comment: Old Shakyamuni set a very poor stage. I want to ask you monks: If Manjusri, who is supposed to have been the teacher of seven Buddhas, could not bring this girl out of meditation, how then could a Bodhisattva who was a mere beginner?

If you understand this intimately, you yourself can enter the great meditation while you are living in the world of delusion.

> *One could not awaken her, the other could.*
> *Neither are good actors.*
> *One wears the mask of god, one a devil's mask.*
> *Had both failed, the drama still would be a comedy.*

短 43. Shuzan's Short Staff

Shuzan held out his short staff and said: 'If you call this a short staff, you oppose its reality. If you do not call it a short staff, you ignore the fact. Now what do you wish to call this?'

Mumon's comment: If you call this a short staff, you oppose its reality. If you do not call it a short staff, you ignore the fact. It cannot be expressed with words and it cannot be expressed without words. Now say quickly what it is.

> *Holding out the short staff,*
> *He gave an order of life or death.*
> *Positive and negative interwoven,*
> *Even Buddhas and patriarchs cannot escape this attack.*

杖 44. *Basho's Staff*

Basho said to his disciple: 'When you have a staff, I will give it to you. If you have no staff, I will take it away from you.'

Mumon's comment: When there is no bridge over the creek the staff will help me. When I return home on a moonless night the staff will accompany me. But if you call this a staff, you will enter hell like an arrow.

> With this staff in my hand
> I can measure the depths and shallows of the world.
> The staff supports the heavens and makes firm the earth.
> Everywhere it goes the true teaching will be spread.

誰 45. Who is He?

Hoen said: 'The past and future Buddhas both are his servants. Who is he?'

Mumon's comment: If you realize clearly who he is, it is as if you met your own father on a busy street. There is no need to ask anyone whether or not your recognition is true.

> *Do not fight with another's bow and arrow.*
> *Do not ride another's horse.*
> *Do not discuss another's faults.*
> *Do not interfere with another's work.*

46. Proceed from the Top of the Pole

Sekiso asked: 'How can you proceed on from the top of a hundred-foot pole?' Another Zen teacher said: 'One who sits on the top of a hundred-foot pole has attained a certain height but still is not handling Zen freely. He should proceed on from there and appear with his whole body in the ten parts of the world.'

Mumon's comment: One can continue his steps or turn his body freely about on the top of the pole. In either case he should be respected. I want to ask you monks, however: How will you proceed from the top of that pole? Look out!

> *The man who lacks the third eye of insight*
> *Will cling to the measure of the hundred feet.*
> *Such a man will jump from there and kill himself,*
> *Like a blind man misleading other blind men.*

關 47. *Three Gates of Tosotsu*

Tosotsu built three barriers and made the monks pass through them. The first barrier is studying Zen. In studying Zen the aim is to see one's own true nature. Now where is your true nature?

Secondly, when one realizes his own true nature he will be free from birth and death. Now when you shut the light from your eyes and become a corpse, how can you free yourself?

Thirdly, if you free yourself from birth and death, you should know where you are. Now your body separates into the four elements. Where are you?

Mumon's comment: Whoever can pass these three barriers will be a master wherever he stands. Whatever happens about him he will turn into Zen.

Otherwise he will be living on poor food and not even enough of that to satisfy himself.

> *An instant realization sees endless time.*
> *Endless time is as one moment.*
> *When one comprehends the endless moment*
> *He realizes the person who is seeing it.*

扇 48. One Road of Kembo

A Zen pupil asked Kembo: 'All Buddhas of the ten parts of the universe enter the one road of Nirvana. Where does that road begin?'

Kembo, raising his walking stick and drawing the figure one in the air, said: 'Here it is.'

This pupil went to Ummon and asked the same question. Ummon, who happened to have a fan in his hand, said: 'This fan will reach to the thirty-third heaven and hit the nose of the presiding deity there. It is like the Dragon Carp of the Eastern Sea tipping over the raincloud with his tail.'

Mumon's comment: One teacher enters the deep sea and scratches the earth and raises dust. The other goes to the mountain top and raises waves that almost touch heaven. One holds, the other gives out. Each supports the profound teaching with a single hand. Kembo and Ummon are like two riders, neither of whom can surpass the other. It is very difficult to find the perfect man. Frankly, neither of them knows where the road starts.

> *Before the first step is taken the goal is reached.*
> *Before the tongue is moved the speech is finished.*
> *More than brilliant intuition is needed*
> *To find the origin of the right road.*

附 49. Amban's Addition

Amban, a layman Zen student, said: 'Mumon has just published forty-eight koans and called the book *Gateless Gate*. He criticizes the old patriarchs' words and actions. I think he is very mischievous. He is like an old doughnut seller trying to catch a passer-by to force his doughnuts down his mouth. The customer can neither swallow nor spit out the doughnuts, and this causes suffering. Mumon has annoyed everyone enough, so I think I shall add one more as a bargain. I wonder if he himself can eat this bargain. If he can, and digest it well, it will be fine, but if not, we will have to put it back into the frying pan with his forty-eight also and cook them again. Mumon, you eat first, before someone else does:

'Buddha, according to a sutra, once said: "Stop, stop. Do not speak. The ultimate truth is not even to think."'

Amban's comment: Where did that so-called teaching come from? How is it that one could not even think it? Suppose someone spoke about it, then what became of it? Buddha himself was a great chatterbox and in this sutra spoke contrarily. Because of this, persons like Mumon appear afterwards in China and make useless doughnuts, annoying people. What shall we do after all? I will show you.

Then Amban put his palms together, folded his hands,

and said: 'Stop, stop. Do not speak. The ultimate truth is not even to think. And now I will make a little circle on the sutra with my finger and add that five thousand other sutras and Vimalakirti's gateless gate all are here!'

If anyone tells you fire is light,
Pay no attention.
When two thieves meet they need no introduction:
They recognize each other without question.

Ten Bulls

by Kekuan [Kaku-an Shi-en]

1. The Search for the Bull

*In the pasture of this world, I endlessly push aside the tall
    grasses in search of the bull.
Following unnamed rivers, lost upon the interpenetrating
    paths of distant mountains,
My strength failing and my vitality exhausted, I cannot find
    the bull.
I only hear the locusts chirring through the forest at night.*

Comment: The bull has been lost. What need is there to
search? Only because of separation from my true nature,
I fail to find him. In the confusion of the senses I lose
even his tracks. Far from home, I see many crossroads,
but which way is the right one I know not. Greed and
fear, good and bad, entangle me.

2. *Discovering the Footprints*

Along the riverbank under the trees, I discover footprints!
Even under the fragrant grass I see his prints.
Deep in remote mountains they are found.
These traces no more can be hidden than one's nose, looking
*   heavenward.*

Comment: Understanding the teaching, I see the footprints of the bull. Then I learn that, just as many utensils are made from one metal, so too are myriad entities made of the fabric of self. Unless I discriminate, how will I perceive the true from the untrue? Not yet having entered the gate, nevertheless I have discerned the path.

3. Perceiving the Bull

I hear the song of the nightingale.
The sun is warm, the wind is mild, willows are green along the
      shore,
Here no bull can hide!
What artist can draw that massive head, those majestic horns?

Comment: When one hears the voice, one can sense its source. As soon as the six senses merge, the gate is entered. Wherever one enters one sees the head of the bull! This unity is like salt in water, like colour in dyestuff. The slightest thing is not apart from self.

4. Catching the Bull

I seize him with a terrific struggle.
His great will and power are inexhaustible.
He charges to the high plateau far above the cloud-mists,
Or in an impenetrable ravine he stands.

Comment: He dwelt in the forest a long time, but I caught him today! Infatuation for scenery interferes with his direction. Longing for sweeter grass, he wanders away. His mind still is stubborn and unbridled. If I wish him to submit, I must raise my whip.

5. Taming the Bull

The whip and rope are necessary,
Else he might stray off down some dusty road.
Being well trained, he becomes naturally gentle.
Then, unfettered, he obeys his master.

Comment: When one thought arises, another thought follows. When the first thought springs from enlightenment, all subsequent thoughts are true. Through delusion, one makes everything untrue. Delusion is not caused by objectivity; it is the result of subjectivity. Hold the nose-ring tight and do not allow even a doubt.

6. Riding the Bull Home

Mounting the bull, slowly I return homeward.
The voice of my flute intones through the evening.
Measuring with hand-beats the pulsating harmony, I direct the
  endless rhythm.
Whoever hears this melody will join me.

Comment: This struggle is over; gain and loss are assimilated. I sing the song of the village woodsman, and play the tunes of the children. Astride the bull, I observe the clouds above. Onward I go, no matter who may wish to call me back.

7. The Bull Transcended

Astride the bull, I reach home.
I am serene. The bull too can rest.
The dawn has come. In blissful repose,
Within my thatched dwelling I have abandoned the whip and
    rope.

Comment: All is one law, not two. We only make the bull a temporary subject. It is as the relation of rabbit and trap, of fish and net. It is as gold and dross, or the moon emerging from a cloud. One path of clear light travels on throughout endless time.

8. Both Bull and Self Transcended

Whip, rope, person, and bull – all merge in No-thing.
This heaven is so vast no message can stain it.
How may a snowflake exist in a raging fire?
Here are the footprints of the patriarchs.

Comment: Mediocrity is gone. Mind is clear of limitation.
I seek no state of enlightenment. Neither do I remain
where no enlightenment exists. Since I linger in neither
condition, eyes cannot see me. If hundreds of birds strew
my path with flowers, such praise would be meaningless.

9. Reaching the Source

*Too many steps have been taken returning to the root and the
source.*
Better to have been blind and deaf from the beginning!
Dwelling in one's true abode, unconcerned with that without –
The river flows tranquilly on and the flowers are red.

Comment: From the beginning, truth is clear. Poised in
silence, I observe the forms of integration and disinte-
gration. One who is not attached to 'form' need not be
'reformed'. The water *is* emerald, the mountain *is* indigo,
and I see that which *is* creating and that which *is*
destroying.

10. *In the World*

Barefooted and naked of breast, I mingle with the people of the
world.
My clothes are ragged and dust-laden and I am ever blissful.
I use no magic to extend my life;
Now, before me, the trees become alive.

Comment: Inside my gate, a thousand sages do not know me. The beauty of my garden is invisible. Why should one search for the footprints of the patriarchs? I go to the market place with my wine bottle and return home with my staff. I visit the wineshop and the market, and everyone I look upon becomes enlightened.

Zen Stories

Some traditional, some by Mujū

空 *A Cup of Tea*

Nan-in, a Japanese master during the Meiji era (1868–1912), received a university professor who came to inquire about Zen.

Nan-in served tea. He poured his visitor's cup full, and then kept on pouring.

The professor watched the overflow until he no longer could restrain himself. 'It is overfull. No more will go in!'

'Like this cup,' Nan-in said, 'you are full of your own opinions and speculations. How can I show you Zen unless you first empty your cup?'

斷 *Is That So?*

The Zen master Hakuin was praised by his neighbours as one living a pure life.

A beautiful Japanese girl whose parents owned a food store lived near him. Suddenly, without any warning, her parents discovered she was with child.

This made her parents angry. She would not confess who the man was, but after much harassment at last named Hakuin.

In great anger the parents went to the master. 'Is that so?' was all he would say.

After the child was born it was brought to Hakuin. By this time he had lost his reputation, which did not trouble him, but he took very good care of the child. He obtained milk from his neighbours and everything else the little one needed.

A year later the girl-mother could stand it no longer. She told her parents the truth – that the real father of the child was a young man who worked in the fishmarket.

The mother and father of the girl at once went to Hakuin to ask his forgiveness, to apologize at length, and to get the child back again.

Hakuin was willing. In yielding the child, all he said was: 'Is that so?'

浪 Great Waves

In the early days of the Meiji era there lived a well-known wrestler called O-nami, Great Waves.

O-nami was immensely strong and knew the art of wrestling. In his private bouts he defeated even his teacher, but in public he was so bashful that his own pupils threw him.

O-nami felt he should go to a Zen master for help. Hakuju, a wandering teacher, was stopping in a little temple nearby, so O-nami went to see him and told him of his trouble.

'Great Waves is your name,' the teacher advised, 'so stay in this temple tonight. Imagine that you are those billows. You are no longer a wrestler who is afraid. You are those huge waves sweeping everything before them, swallowing all in their path. Do this and you will be the greatest wrestler in the land.'

The teacher retired. O-nami sat in meditation trying to imagine himself as waves. He thought of many different things. Then gradually he turned more and more to the feelings of the waves. As the night advanced the waves became larger and larger. They swept away the flowers in their vases. Even the Buddha in the shrine was inundated. Before dawn the temple was nothing but the ebb and flow of an immense sea.

In the morning the teacher found O-nami meditating,

a faint smile on his face. He patted the wrestler's shoulder. 'Now nothing can disturb you,' he said. 'You are those waves. You will sweep everything before you.'

The same day O-nami entered the wrestling contests and won. After that, no one in Japan was able to defeat him.

難 *Muddy Road*

Tanzan and Ekido were once travelling together down a muddy road. A heavy rain was still falling.

Coming around a bend, they met a lovely girl in a silk kimono and sash, unable to cross the intersection.

'Come on, girl,' said Tanzan at once. Lifting her in his arms, he carried her over the mud.

Ekido did not speak again until that night when they reached a lodging temple. Then he no longer could restrain himself. 'We monks don't go near females,' he told Tanzan, 'especially not young and lovely ones. It is dangerous. Why did you do that?'

'I left the girl there,' said Tanzan. 'Are you still carrying her?'

絶 A Parable

Buddha told a parable in a sutra:

A man travelling across a field encountered a tiger. He fled, the tiger after him. Coming to a precipice, he caught hold of the root of a wild vine and swung himself down over the edge. The tiger sniffed at him from above. Trembling, the man looked down to where, far below, another tiger was waiting to eat him. Only the vine sustained him.

Two mice, one white and one black, little by little started to gnaw away the vine. The man saw a luscious strawberry near him. Grasping the vine with one hand, he plucked the strawberry with the other. How sweet it tasted!

音 The Sound of One Hand

The master of Kennin temple was Mokurai, Silent Thunder. He had a little protégé named Toyo who was only twelve years old. Toyo saw the older disciples visit the master's room each morning and evening to receive instruction in sanzen or personal guidance in which they were given koans to stop mind-wandering.

Toyo wished to do sanzen also.

'Wait a while,' said Mokurai. 'You are too young.'

But the child insisted, so the teacher finally consented.

In the evening little Toyo went at the proper time to the threshold of Mokurai's sanzen room. He struck the gong to announce his presence, bowed respectfully three times outside the door, and went to sit before the master in respectful silence.

'You can hear the sound of two hands when they clap together,' said Mokurai. 'Now show me the sound of one hand.'

Toyo bowed and went to his room to consider this problem. From his window he could hear the music of the geishas. 'Ah, I have it!' he proclaimed.

The next evening, when his teacher asked him to illustrate the sound of one hand, Toyo began to play the music of the geishas.

'No, no,' said Mokurai. 'That will never do. That is not the sound of one hand. You've not got it at all.'

Thinking that such music might interrupt, Toyo moved his abode to a quiet place. He meditated again. 'What can the sound of one hand be?' He happened to hear some water dripping. 'I have it,' imagined Toyo.

When he next appeared before his teacher, Toyo imitated dripping water.

'What is that?' asked Mokurai. 'That is the sound of dripping water, but not the sound of one hand. Try again.'

In vain Toyo meditated to hear the sound of one hand. He heard the sighing of the wind. But the sound was rejected.

He heard the cry of an owl. This also was refused.

The sound of one hand was not the locusts.

For more than ten times Toyo visited Mokurai with different sounds. All were wrong. For almost a year he pondered what the sound of one hand might be.

At last little Toyo entered true meditation and transcended all sounds. 'I could collect no more,' he explained later, 'so I reached the soundless sound.'

Toyo had realized the sound of one hand.

經 *Reciting Sutras*

A farmer requested a Tendai priest to recite sutras for his wife, who had died. After the recitation was over the farmer asked: 'Do you think my wife will gain merit from this?'

'Not only your wife, but all sentient beings will benefit from the recitation of sutras,' answered the priest.

'If you say all sentient beings will benefit,' said the farmer, 'my wife may be very weak and others will take advantage of her, getting the benefit she should have. So please recite sutras just for her.'

The priest explained that it was the desire of a Buddhist to offer blessings and wish merit for every living being.

'That is a fine teaching,' concluded the farmer, 'but please make one exception. I have a neighbour who is rough and mean to me. Just exclude him from all those sentient beings.'

宣 *Trading Dialogue for Lodging*

Provided he makes and wins an argument about Buddhism with those who live there, any wandering monk can remain in a Zen temple. If he is defeated, he has to move on.

In a temple in the northern part of Japan two brother monks were dwelling together. The elder one was learned, but the younger one was stupid and had but one eye.

A wandering monk came and asked for lodging, properly challenging them to a debate about the sublime teaching. The elder brother, tired that day from much studying, told the younger one to take his place. 'Go and request the dialogue in silence,' he cautioned.

So the young monk and the stranger went to the shrine and sat down.

Shortly afterwards the traveller rose and went in to the elder brother and said: 'Your young brother is a wonderful fellow. He defeated me.'

'Relate the dialogue to me,' said the elder one.

'Well,' explained the traveller, 'first I held up one finger, representing Buddha, the enlightened one. So he held up two fingers, signifying Buddha and his teaching. I held up three fingers, representing Buddha, his teaching, and his followers, living the harmonious life. Then he shook his clenched fist in my face, indicating that all three come from one realization. Thus he won and so I have no right to remain here.' With this, the traveller left.

'Where is that fellow?' asked the younger one, running in to his elder brother.

'I understand you won the debate.'

'Won nothing. I'm going to beat him up.'

'Tell me the subject of the debate,' asked the elder one.

'Why, the minute he saw me he held up one finger, insulting me by insinuating that I have only one eye. Since he was a stranger I thought I would be polite to him, so I held up two fingers, congratulating him that he has two eyes. Then the impolite wretch held up three fingers, suggesting that between us we only have three eyes. So I got mad and started to punch him, but he ran out and that ended it!'

元 Gisho's Work

Gisho was ordained as a nun when she was ten years old. She received training just as the little boys did. When she reached the age of sixteen she travelled from one Zen master to another, studying with them all.

She remained three years with Unzan, six years with Gukei, but was unable to obtain a clear vision. At last she went to the master Inzan.

Inzan showed her no distinction at all on account of her sex. He scolded her like a thunderstorm. He cuffed her to awaken her inner nature.

Gisho remained with Inzan thirteen years, and then she found that which she was seeking!

In her honour, Inzan wrote a poem:

> This nun studied thirteen years under my guidance.
> In the evening she considered the deepest koans,
> In the morning she was wrapped in other koans.
> The Chinese nun Tetsuma surpassed all before her,
> And since Mujaku none has been so genuine as this Gisho!
> Yet there are many more gates for her to pass through.
> She should receive still more blows from my iron fist.

After Gisho was enlightened she went to the province of Banshu, started her own Zen temple, and taught two hundred other nuns until she passed away one year in the month of August.

謙 *The Giver Should be Thankful*

While Seisetsu was the master of Engaku in Kamakura he required larger quarters, since those in which he was teaching were overcrowded. Umezu Seibei, a merchant of Edo, decided to donate five hundred pieces of gold called ryo toward the construction of a more commodious school. This money he brought to the teacher.

Seisetsu said: 'All right. I will take it.'

Umezu gave Seisetsu the sack of gold, but he was dissatisfied with the attitude of the teacher. One might live a whole year on three ryo, and the merchant had not even been thanked for five hundred.

'In that sack are five hundred ryo,' hinted Umezu.

'You told me that before,' replied Seisetsu.

'Even if I am a wealthy merchant, five hundred ryo is a lot of money,' said Umezu.

'Do you want me to thank you for it?' asked Seisetsu.

'You ought to,' replied Umezu.

'Why should I?' inquired Seisetsu. 'The giver should be thankful.'

道 *The True Path*

Just before Ninakawa passed away the Zen master Ikkyu visited him. 'Shall I lead you on?' Ikkyu asked.

Ninakawa replied: 'I came here alone and I go alone. What help could you be to me?'

Ikkyu answered: 'If you think you really come and go, that is your delusion. Let me show you the path on which there is no coming and no going.'

With his words, Ikkyu had revealed the path so clearly that Ninakawa smiled and passed away.

門 The Gates of Paradise

A soldier named Nobushige came to Hakuin, and asked: 'Is there really a paradise and a hell?'

'Who are you?' inquired Hakuin.

'I am a samurai,' the warrior replied.

'You, a soldier!' exclaimed Hakuin. 'What kind of ruler would have you as his guard? Your face looks like that of a beggar.'

Nobushige became so angry that he began to draw his sword, but Hakuin continued: 'So you have a sword! Your weapon is probably much too dull to cut off my head.'

As Nobushige drew his sword Hakuin remarked: 'Here open the gates of hell!'

At these words the samurai, perceiving the master's discipline, sheathed his sword and bowed.

'Here open the gates of paradise,' said Hakuin.

路 *The Tunnel*

Zenkai, the son of a samurai, journeyed to Edo and there became the retainer of a high official. He fell in love with the official's wife and was discovered. In self-defence, he slew the official. Then he ran away with the wife.

Both of them later became thieves. But the woman was so greedy that Zenkai grew disgusted. Finally, leaving her, he journeyed far away to the province of Buzen, where he became a wandering mendicant.

To atone for his past, Zenkai resolved to accomplish some good deed in his lifetime. Knowing of a dangerous road over a cliff that had caused the death and injury of many persons, he resolved to cut a tunnel through the mountains there.

Begging food in the daytime, Zenkai worked at night digging his tunnel. When thirty years had gone by, the tunnel was 2,280 feet long, 20 feet high, and 30 feet wide.

Two years before the work was completed, the son of the official he had slain, who was a skilful swordsman, found Zenkai out and came to kill him in revenge.

'I will give you my life willingly,' said Zenkai. 'Only let me finish this work. On the day it is completed, then you may kill me.'

So the son awaited the day. Several months passed and Zenkai kept on digging. The son grew tired of doing nothing and began to help with the digging. After he had helped for more than a year, he came to admire Zenkai's strong will and character.

At last the tunnel was completed and the people could use it and travel in safety.

'Now cut off my head,' said Zenkai. 'My work is done.'

'How can I cut off my own teacher's head?' asked the younger man with tears in his eyes.

猫
頭
*The Most Valuable Thing
in the World*

Sozan, a Chinese Zen master, was asked by a student:
'What is the most valuable thing in the world?'

The master replied: 'The head of a dead cat.'

'Why is the head of a dead cat the most valuable thing
in the world?' inquired the student.

Sozan replied: 'Because no one can name its price.'

默 *Learning to be Silent*

The pupils of the Tendai school used to study meditation before Zen entered Japan. Four of them who were intimate friends promised one another to observe seven days of silence.

On the first day all were silent. Their meditation had begun auspiciously, but when night came and the oil-lamps were growing dim one of the pupils could not help exclaiming to a servant: 'Fix those lamps.'

The second pupil was surprised to hear the first one talk. 'We are not supposed to say a word,' he remarked.

'You two are stupid. Why did you talk?' asked the third.

'I am the only one who has not talked,' concluded the fourth pupil.

茶 Real Prosperity

A rich man asked Sengai to write something for the continued prosperity of his family so that it might be treasured from generation to generation.

Sengai obtained a large sheet of paper and wrote: 'Father dies, son dies, grandson dies.'

The rich man became angry. 'I asked you to write something for the happiness of my family! Why do you make such a joke as this?'

'No joke is intended,' explained Sengai. 'If before you yourself die your son should die, this would grieve you greatly. If your grandson should pass away before your son, both of you would be broken-hearted. If your family, generation after generation, passes away in the order I have named, it will be the natural course of life. I call this real prosperity.'

逍 *Incense Burner*

A woman of Nagasaki named Kame was one of the few makers of incense burners in Japan. Such a burner is a work of art to be used only in a tearoom or before a family shrine.

Kame, whose father before her had been such an artist, was fond of drinking. She also smoked and associated with men most of the time. Whenever she made a little money she gave a feast inviting artists, poets, carpenters, workers, men of many vocations and avocations. In their association she evolved her designs.

Kame was exceedingly slow in creating, but when her work was finished it was always a masterpiece. Her burners were treasured in homes whose womenfolk never drank, smoked, or associated freely with men.

The mayor of Nagasaki once requested Kame to design an incense burner for him. She delayed doing so until almost half a year had passed. At that time the mayor, who had been promoted to office in a distant city, visited her. He urged Kame to begin work on his burner.

At last receiving the inspiration, Kame made the incense burner. After it was completed she placed it upon a table. She looked at it long and carefully. She smoked and drank before it as if it were her own company. All day she observed it.

At last, picking up a hammer, Kame smashed it to bits. She saw it was not the perfect creation her mind demanded.

敵 The Taste of Banzo's Sword

Matajuro Yagyu was the son of a famous swordsman. His father, believing that his son's work was too mediocre to anticipate mastership, disowned him.

So Matajuro went to Mount Futara and there found the famous swordsman Banzo. But Banzo confirmed the father's judgement. 'You wish to learn swordsmanship under my guidance?' asked Banzo. 'You cannot fulfil the requirements.'

'But if I work hard, how many years will it take me to become a master?' persisted the youth.

'The rest of your life,' replied Banzo.

'I cannot wait that long,' explained Matajuro. 'I am willing to pass through any hardship if only you will teach me. If I become your devoted servant, how long might it be?'

'Oh, maybe ten years,' Banzo relented.

'My father is getting old, and soon I must take care of him,' continued Matajuro. 'If I work far more intensively, how long would it take me?'

'Oh, maybe thirty years,' said Banzo.

'Why is that?' asked Matajuro. 'First you say ten and now thirty years. I will undergo any hardship to master this art in the shortest time!'

'Well,' said Banzo, 'in that case you will have to remain with me for seventy years. A man in such a hurry as you are to get results seldom learns quickly.'

'Very well,' declared the youth, understanding at last that he was being rebuked for impatience, 'I agree.'

Matajuro was told never to speak of fencing and never to touch a sword. He cooked for his master, washed the dishes, made his bed, cleaned the yard, cared for the garden, all without a word of swordsmanship.

Three years passed. Still Matajuro laboured on. Thinking of his future, he was sad. He had not even begun to learn the art to which he had devoted his life.

But one day Banzo crept up behind him and gave him a terrific blow with a wooden sword.

The following day, when Matajuro was cooking rice, Banzo again sprang upon him unexpectedly.

After that, day and night, Matajuro had to defend himself from unexpected thrusts. Not a moment passed in any day that he did not have to think of the taste of Banzo's sword.

He learned so rapidly he brought smiles to the face of his master. Matajuro became the greatest swordsman in the land.

雪 *A Letter to a Dying Man*

Bassui wrote the following letter to one of his disciples who was about to die:

'The essence of your mind is not born, so it will never die. It is not an existence, which is perishable. It is not an emptiness, which is a mere void. It has neither colour nor form. It enjoys no pleasures and suffers no pains.

'I know you are very ill. Like a good Zen student, you are facing that sickness squarely. You may not know exactly who is suffering, but question yourself: What is the essence of this mind? Think only of this. You will need no more. Covet nothing. Your end which is endless is as a snowflake dissolving in the pure air.'

究 Teaching the Ultimate

In early times in Japan, bamboo-and-paper lanterns were used with candles inside. A blind man, visiting a friend one night, was offered a lantern to carry home with him.

'I do not need a lantern,' he said. 'Darkness or light is all the same to me.'

'I know you do not need a lantern to find your way,' his friend replied, 'but if you don't have one, someone else may run into you. So you must take it.'

The blind man started off with the lantern and before he had walked very far someone ran squarely into him. 'Look out where you are going!' he exclaimed to the stranger. 'Can't you see this lantern?'

'Your candle has burned out, brother,' replied the stranger.

黙 *The Silent Temple*

Shoichi was a one-eyed teacher of Zen, sparkling with enlightenment. He taught his disciples in Tofuku temple.

Day and night the whole temple stood in silence. There was no sound at all.

Even the reciting of sutras was abolished by the teacher. His pupils had nothing to do but meditate.

When the master passed away, an old neighbour heard the ringing of bells and the recitation of sutras. Then she knew Shoichi had gone.

THE STORY OF PENGUIN CLASSICS

Before 1946 ...'Classics' are mainly the domain of academics and students, without readable editions for everyone else. This all changes when a little-known classicist, E. V. Rieu, presents Penguin founder Allen Lane with the translation of Homer's *Odyssey* that he has been working on and reading to his wife Nelly in his spare time.

1946 The *Odyssey* becomes the first Penguin Classic published, and promptly sells three million copies. Suddenly, classic books are no longer for the privileged few.

1950s Rieu, now series editor, turns to professional writers for the best modern, readable translations, including Dorothy L. Sayers's *Inferno* and Robert Graves's *The Twelve Caesars*, which revives the salacious original.

1960s 1961 sees the arrival of the Penguin Modern Classics, showcasing the best twentieth-century writers from around the world. Rieu retires in 1964, hailing the Penguin Classics list as 'the greatest educative force of the 20th century'.

1970s A new generation of translators arrives to swell the Penguin Classics ranks, and the list grows to encompass more philosophy, religion, science, history and politics.

1980s The Penguin American Library joins the Classics stable, with titles such as *The Last of the Mohicans* safeguarded. Penguin Classics now offers the most comprehensive library of world literature available.

1990s Penguin Popular Classics are launched, offering readers budget editions of the greatest works of literature. Penguin Audiobooks brings the classics to a listening audience for the first time, and in 1999 the launch of the Penguin Classics website takes them online to an ever larger global readership.

The 21st Century Penguin Classics are rejacketed for the first time in nearly twenty years. This world famous series now consists of more than 1,300 titles, making the widest range of the best books ever written available to millions – and constantly redefining the meaning of what makes a 'classic'.

The Odyssey continues ...

The best books ever written

PENGUIN ⚫ CLASSICS

SINCE 1946